The Paper Planes Club

Written by Zoë Clarke

Illustrated by Warwick Johnson Cadwell

Collins

Lenny liked living at the top of his giant tower block.

On a sunny day, Lenny could see for miles!

But the best thing was the tower block nearby.
By day, he could see some of the people in some
of the windows.

By night, he was able to see different people in different windows.

One day Lenny spotted a girl and a very large dog in one of the windows. He waved. She waved back.

Lenny ripped a page out of his pad and scribbled a note.

He folded the page and made a paper plane.
He threw it from the window and watched it fly!

The paper plane did a gentle loop and landed near the girl's window.

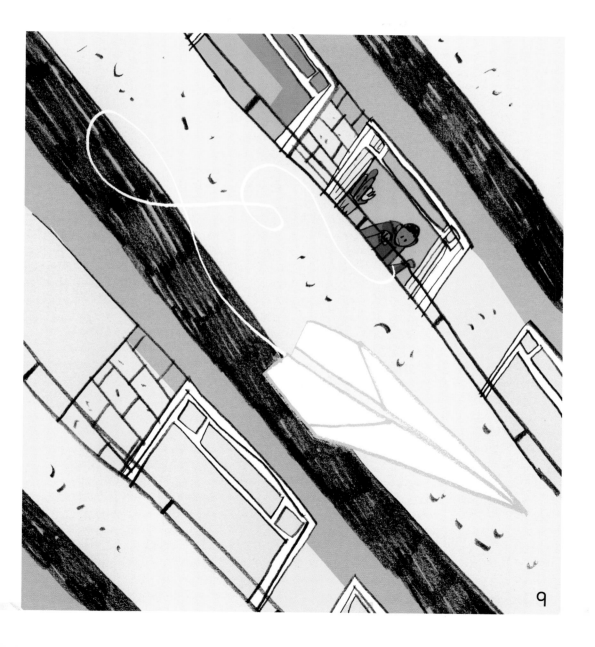

The girl fetched the paper plane from the ledge.

What are your names?

The girl drew a picture on a huge sheet of paper and stuck it to her window.

Lenny folded another plane, but this time the wind snatched the plane and pushed it in front of another window!

An old man picked it up.

The old man put a photo in his window with a note.

Marley made his own paper plane. He said he liked Lenny's plant.

Lenny put a note in his window.

Soon, the air was full of paper planes, flying from one tower block to the other.

There were yellow planes and blue planes.
There were little planes and large planes.

Some planes had notes, some had pictures.

Some planes landed on the phone cables, like strange paper birds from a faraway land.

People stuck up pictures and notes to show they were part of the Paper Planes Club.

Giant tower blocks saying hello to each other,
and the world.

Join the Paper Planes Club

After reading

Letters and Sounds: Phase 5

Word count: 300

Focus phonemes: /ai/ a /ee/ ey, e, y /oo/ u /igh/ y, ie /ch/ tch, t /j/ g, ge, dge /l/ le /f/ ph /w/ wh

Common exception words: of, to, the, are, said, one, were, people

Curriculum links: Science: Everyday materials; Art and design; PSHE

National Curriculum learning objectives: Reading/word reading: apply phonic knowledge and skills as the route to decode words, read other words of more than one syllable that contain taught GPCs; Reading/comprehension: drawing on what they already know or on background information and vocabulary provided by the teacher

Developing fluency

- Your child may enjoy hearing you read the book.
- Take turns to read the main text. Check that your child reads the words in the pictures too.

Phonic practice

- Focus on the /j/ and /igh/ sounds. Challenge your child to find a word (or words) containing the /j/ sound on the following pages:

  page 2 (*giant*)　　page 9 (*gentle*)　　page 10 (*ledge*)　　page 19 (*strange*)
- Repeat for /igh/ on these pages:

  page 4 (*nearby*)　　page 5 (*by, night*)　　page 16 (*flying*)

Extending vocabulary

- Ask your child to think of a sentence which includes these words:

  sun　　　fly　　　land　　　gentle
- Can your child think of new sentences using the same words but with a different ending?

  sunny　　　flying　　　landed　　　gently